SUPER SIMPLE
ENGINEERING PROJECTS

ENGINEER IT!

SKYSCRAPER

PROJECTS

CAROLYN BERNHARDT

CONSULTING EDITOR, DIANE CRAIG, M.A./READING SPECIALIST

Super Sandcastle

An Imprint of Abdo Publishing
abdopublishing.com

abdopublishing.com

Published by Abdo Publishing, a division of ABDO, PO Box 398166, Minneapolis, Minnesota 55439. Copyright © 2018 by Abdo Consulting Group, Inc. International copyrights reserved in all countries. No part of this book may be reproduced in any form without written permission from the publisher. Super SandCastle™ is a trademark and logo of Abdo Publishing.

Printed in the United States of America, North Mankato, Minnesota
062017
092017

THIS BOOK CONTAINS
RECYCLED MATERIALS

Production: Mighty Media, Inc.
Editor: Liz Salzmann
Cover Photographs: Mighty Media, Inc.; Shutterstock
Interior Photographs: Mighty Media, Inc.; Shutterstock; Wikimedia Commons/public domain

The following manufacturers/names appearing in this book are trademarks:
Artist's Loft™, Crayola®, Nutella®, Play-Doh®, Scotch®

Publisher's Cataloging-in-Publication Data

Names: Bernhardt, Carolyn, author.
Title: Engineer it! skyscraper projects / by Carolyn Bernhardt.
Other titles: Skyscraper projects
Description: Minneapolis, MN : Abdo Publishing, 2018. | Series: Super simple
    engineering projects
Identifiers: LCCN 2016963083 | ISBN 9781532111266 (lib. bdg.) |
    ISBN 9781680789119 (ebook)
Subjects: LCSH: Skyscrapers--Juvenile literature. | Skyscrapers--Design and
    construction--Juvenile literature. | Structural engineering--Juvenile literature.
Classification: DDC 690--dc23
LC record available at http://lccn.loc.gov/2016963083

Super SandCastle™ books are created by a team of professional educators, reading specialists, and content developers around five essential components—phonemic awareness, phonics, vocabulary, text comprehension, and fluency—to assist young readers as they develop reading skills and strategies and increase their general knowledge. All books are written, reviewed, and leveled for guided reading and early reading intervention programs for use in shared, guided, and independent reading and writing activities to support a balanced approach to literacy instruction.

TO ADULT HELPERS

The projects in this title are fun and simple. There are just a few things to remember. Kids may be using messy materials such as glue or paint. Make sure they protect their clothes and work surfaces. Review the projects before starting, and be ready to assist when necessary.

CONTENTS

WHAT IS A SKYSCRAPER?

A skyscraper is a very tall building. You might think that any very tall structure is a skyscraper. But that is not true. Skyscrapers have certain features.

A skyscraper has to have many stories. It must also have walls so people can live or work inside it. Tall structures such as monuments or water towers are not skyscrapers. A skyscraper also has to be taller than the buildings near it, so it stands out.

NOT A SKYSCRAPER

SKYSCRAPER

HOME INSURANCE BUILDING

People started building skyscrapers in the 1880s. The first skyscraper was the Home Insurance Building in Chicago, Illinois. It opened in 1885 and was ten stories tall. That is not very tall for a building now. But at the time, there were few buildings that tall. Then, people kept building taller and taller buildings. Today's skyscrapers are at least 40 stories tall. Some have more than 100 stories!

BURJ KHALIFA

The tallest building in the world was completed in 2010. It is the Burj Khalifa in the city of Dubai in the United Arab Emirates. The Burj Khalifa has 163 stories. It is 2,717 feet (828 m) tall. This skyscraper has hotel rooms, apartments, offices, and restaurants.

HOW PEOPLE USE
SKYSCRAPERS

Skyscrapers have three main uses. These are manufacturing, business, and housing. Some skyscrapers have more than one of these uses.

MANUFACTURING

Many of the first skyscrapers helped increase manufacturing. These buildings were factories and **warehouses**. They had more room for the machines and supplies needed to produce goods. There was also more room to store the finished products. This meant that more goods could be produced.

BUSINESS

Skyscrapers helped businesses grow. Companies could provide offices for many employees in one building. This was easier than buying or building additional office buildings as a company grew.

HOUSING

Hotels and apartments are common uses for skyscrapers. These buildings can house many people on a small plot of land. In cities, this helps more people live closer to where their jobs are.

BUILDING
SKYSCRAPERS

Up until the mid-1800s, most buildings were made of stone and brick. But these materials are too heavy to use for really tall buildings. The upper floors would crush the lower floors.

During the 1800s, steel became easier and cheaper to make. Builders figured out that steel could be used as a framework for tall buildings. This framework was called a skeleton.

Outer walls were then **attached** to the skeleton. The steel skeleton, rather than the walls, supported the building.

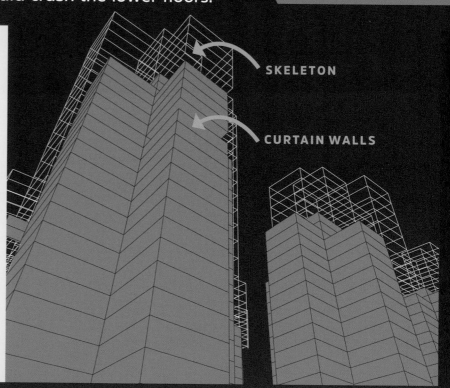

SKELETON

CURTAIN WALLS

THE EMPIRE STATE BUILDING

From 1930 to 1931, there was a contest in New York City to build the world's tallest building. The winner was the Empire State Building. It has 102 stories and is 1,250 feet (381 m) tall. The Empire State Building was completed in 1931. It was the tallest building in the world until 1972.

A skyscraper's outer walls are called **curtain** walls. This is because they hang from the skeleton like curtains. The first curtain walls were made of stone. Today, they are usually made of metal and glass.

GOING UP!

The elevator was invented in the 1850s. This made getting from floor to floor easier, so taller buildings became more practical.

MATERIALS

Here are some of the materials that you will need for the projects in this book.

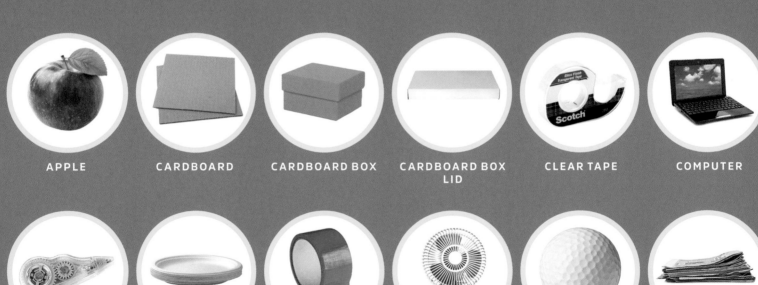

APPLE

CARDBOARD

CARDBOARD BOX

CARDBOARD BOX LID

CLEAR TAPE

COMPUTER

CORRECTION TAPE

DISPOSABLE PLATES

DUCT TAPE

ELECTRIC FAN

GOLF BALL

NEWSPAPER

NUTELLA

PAINT

PAINTBRUSHES

**PAPER-TOWEL
TUBES**

PENCIL

PLAY-DOH

PRINTER

PUSHPINS

RULER

SCISSORS

**SCRAPBOOK
PAPER**

STRING

**TOILET-PAPER
TUBE**

TOOTHPICK

WAFFLE PRETZELS

**WOODEN CRAFT
STICKS**

**WOODEN
SKEWERS**

**WRAPPING-PAPER
TUBE**

PAPERSCRAPER

MATERIALS: colorful scrapbook paper, ruler, scissors, pencil, clear tape

Did you know that something as flimsy as paper can be strong? This is possible if it is in the right shape! A triangle is the strongest shape in **architecture**. Builders often use triangles in skyscraper skeletons. The more triangles there are, the stronger the structure will be.

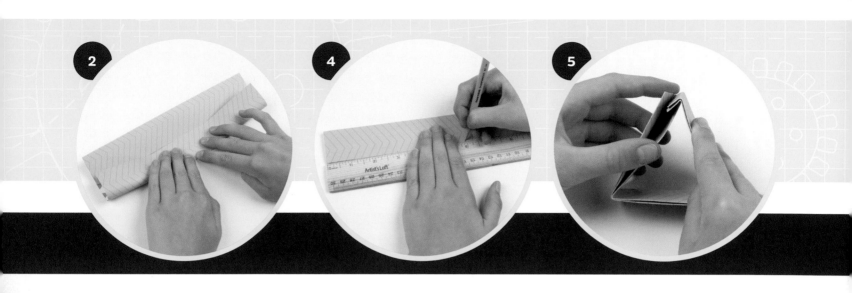

① Cut a rectangle out of paper. Make it 9½ by 6 inches (24 by 15 cm).

② Fold the rectangle in half **lengthwise**. Unfold the paper and fold both long sides to the center fold.

③ Refold the paper on the center fold to make a long strip. The flaps should be inside the fold.

④ Starting at one end of the paper strip, make a mark every 3 inches (7.5 cm).

⑤ Fold the paper on the marks to form a triangle. Tuck the short tab on one end between the folds on the other end. Use tape to hold it in place.

⑥ Repeat steps 1 through 5 to make more triangles.

⑦ **Stack** the triangles into a skyscraper or other structure. Set objects on it to see how much weight it will hold!

TOOTHPICK
TOWER

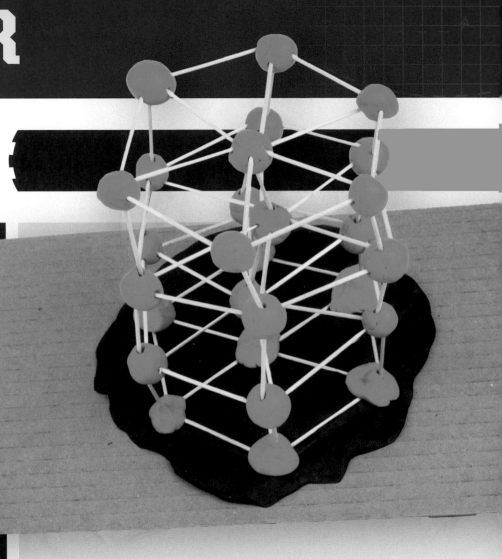

MATERIALS: cardboard, 2 colors of Play-Doh, toothpicks

You don't need a lot of different materials to build something strong and beautiful. You just need creativity! Many buildings around the world are made out of only a few types of materials. Concrete, metal, and glass are common materials used in today's skyscrapers.

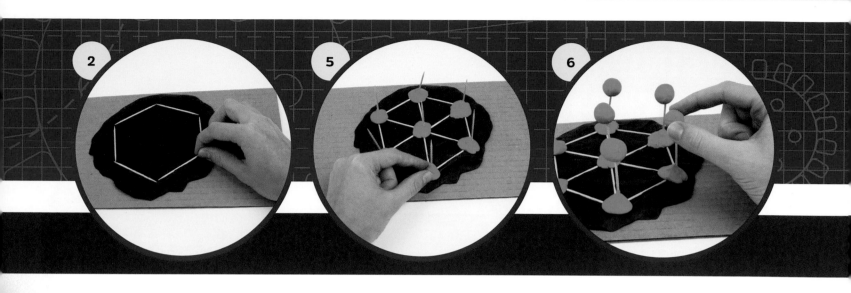

1. Press one color of Play-Doh into a layer on the cardboard. This is your building's base.

2. Set toothpicks on the base to outline your building's shape. This is the bottom of the building.

3. At each spot two toothpicks meet, stick a toothpick vertically through the Play-Doh base and into the cardboard.

4. Roll the second color of Play-Doh into small balls.

5. Press balls of Play-Doh around the ends of the toothpicks where they meet.

6. Press a Play-Doh ball on top of each vertical toothpick.

7. Connect the Play-Doh balls with toothpicks.

8. Use Play-Doh and toothpicks to add more stories to your skyscraper. See how tall you can make it before it falls over.

SKYLINE CYLINDERS

MATERIALS: computer, printer, wrapping-paper tubes, toilet-paper tubes, paper-towel tubes, scissors, newspaper, paint, paintbrush, correction tape

A skyline is the outline of buildings against the sky. No two cities have the same skyline. A city's skyscrapers can make its skyline easy to recognize.

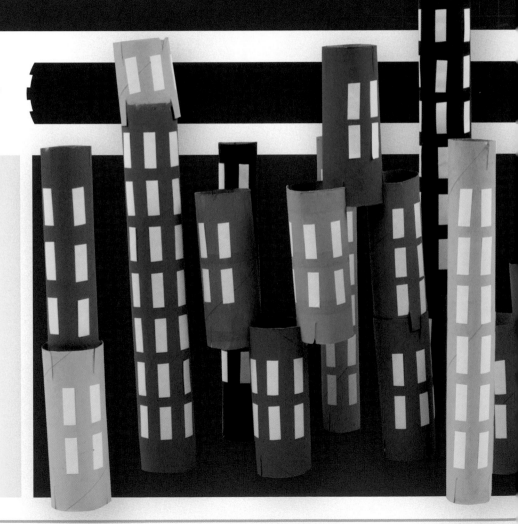

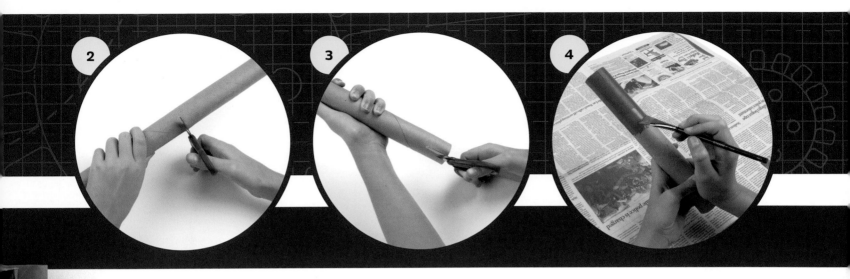

1　Have an adult help you **research** city skylines **online**. Print out pictures of some of your favorites. Use them as inspiration!

2　Cut the cardboard tubes into pieces of various lengths.

3　Cut four short **slits** into both ends of each tube. Space the slits evenly.

4　Cover your work surface with newspaper. Paint the tube pieces different colors. Let the paint dry.

Continued on the next page.

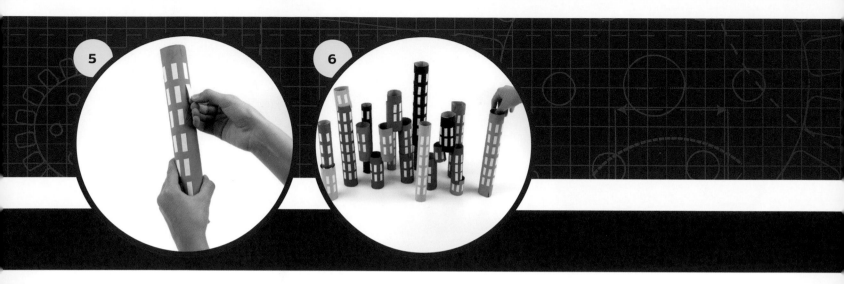

SKYLINE CYLINDERS (CONTINUED)

5 Use correction tape to add windows to your skyscrapers. Or you could paint the windows.

6 Arrange the tubes to form a city skyline. Use the **slits** to **stack** tubes on top of each other. Try copying famous skylines or make up your own super skyline!

DIGGING DEEPER

When **designing** a skyscraper, something the **architect** thinks about is its effect on the city's skyline. A city's skyline is part of its **identity**. So, any changes to it are taken very seriously. The architect makes drawings and models that include the planned skyscraper and all of the buildings around it. Then city planners can see the proposed changes and decide whether to approve the new skyscraper.

BRICK AND MORTAR
BUILD

MATERIALS: Nutella, disposable plate, wooden craft stick, waffle pretzels, apple, string, notebook, pencil

Did you know that bricks were the very first human-made building materials? People have built brick structures for thousands of years! Bricks are held together by mortar. Mortar can be made of different materials, including mud, clay, and cement.

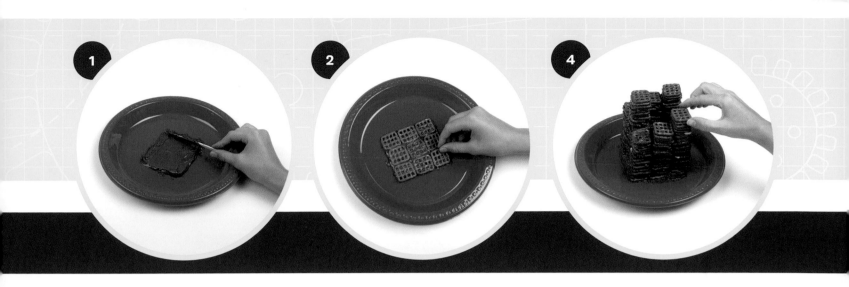

1 Spread a square layer of Nutella on the plate with the craft stick. Make the square big enough for nine waffle pretzels to fit on it. The Nutella represents the mortar.

2 Press nine pretzels into the Nutella layer. Make three rows of three pretzels. The pretzels represent bricks.

3 Spread a layer of mortar on top of the bricks. Add bricks on top of the eight outer bricks to start building towers.

4 Keep adding layers of mortar and bricks to the eight towers. Build them up until they are as tall as you want them to be.

Continued on the next page.

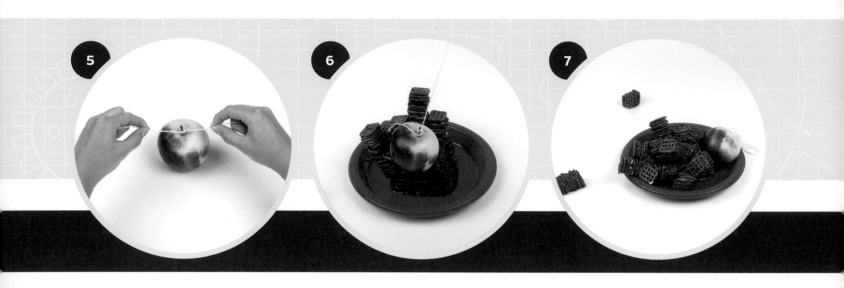

BRICK AND MORTAR BUILD (CONTINUED)

5 Tie a piece of string to the apple's stem.

6 Swing the apple into your towers like a wrecking ball.

7 Write what happened down in a notebook. Where were your buildings the weakest? What broke? What stayed together?

8 Invite some friends over for a snack!

DIGGING DEEPER

Bricks are an excellent building material. They can withstand bad weather as well as fire. Bricks are made out of clay. Then they are exposed to very high heat. This makes them very strong. Mortar is the glue that holds bricks together. It is applied when it is wet. When the mortar dries, it holds the bricks firmly in place. It also creates a seal between the bricks. However, mortar is not as strong as brick. So, it needs to be maintained and repaired regularly. Otherwise, the bricks will fall apart over time.

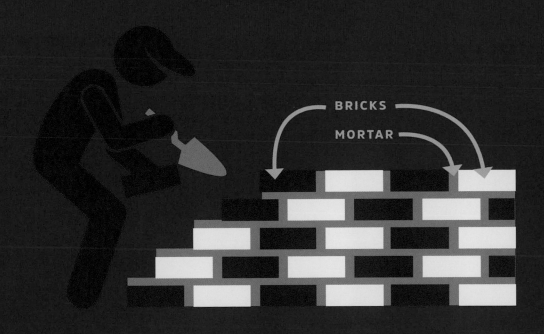

BRICKS

MORTAR

STACK
TO THE SKY

MATERIALS: cardboard boxes, toilet-paper tubes, duct tape, scissors, paint, paintbrush

Engineers and **architects** experiment with different shapes, sizes, and weights of building materials. This helps them find new ways to **design** strong skyscrapers.

① Cover the boxes and tubes with duct tape or paint.

② Set a few larger boxes next to each other to form the base of your skyscraper.

③ **Stack** the tubes and other boxes on the base to create your skyscraper. Try different arrangements to make a tall, sturdy building.

DIGGING DEEPER

Skyscrapers are often checked after they are built. Over time, wind, storms, and other elements can **damage** buildings. It is important to make sure that they remain safe. Engineers check the outsides of buildings for cracks and other problems. Most engineers do this from **scaffolds** that are lowered from the roof. But some engineers **rappel** down buildings to check for problems!

WINDPROOF
BUILDING

MATERIALS: newspaper, cardboard box lid, paint, paintbrush, scrapbook paper, ruler, pencil, scissors, clear tape, wooden skewers, pushpin, cardboard, golf ball, electric fan

Wind is a strong force! Skyscrapers are built to sway a little with the wind so they don't break. These tall structures need to be both strong and **flexible**.

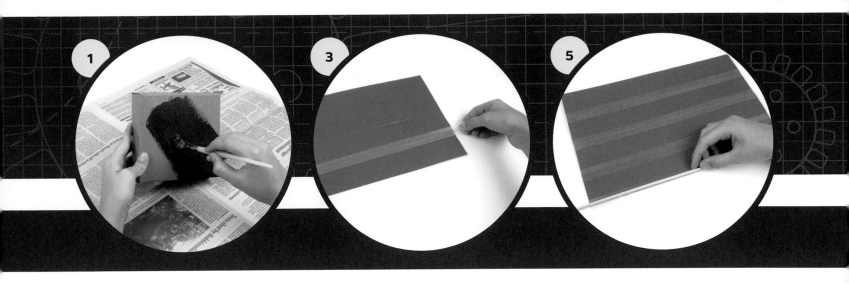

1. Cover your work surface with newspaper. Paint the box lid. Let the paint dry.

2. Cut four strips of scrapbook paper. Make each strip 12 by 2 inches (30 by 5 cm).

3. Lay the strips side by side. Tape them together.

4. Place a skewer along one of the long edges. Make sure the pointed end sticks out past the side.

5. Tape the skewer in place. Wrap the tape over the skewer so it sticks to both sides of the paper.

Continued on the next page.

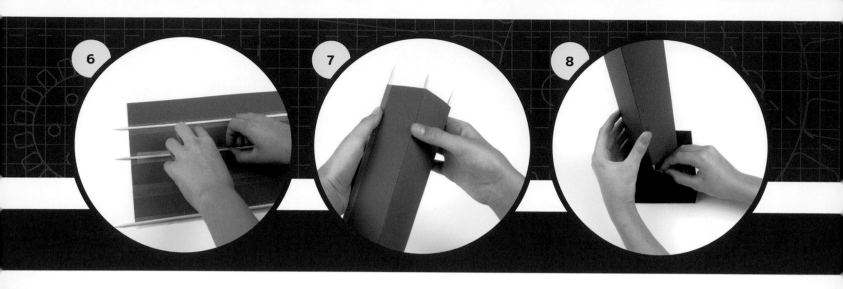

WINDPROOF BUILDING (CONTINUED)

6 Tape a skewer along each taped **seam**. Make sure all the points stick out the same distance past the edge. Pinch the tape around each skewer to hold it in place.

7 Fold the paper at the seams. The skewers should be on the inside. Tape the edges together. This is your skyscraper.

8 Set the skyscraper on the box lid. Use the pushpin to poke a hole in the lid at each skewer.

9 Push the skewers into the pushpin holes. Your skyscraper should stand up straight.

10 Cut a square out of cardboard. Make it 1⅞ inches (4.8 cm) on each side. Place it inside the building so it rests on top of the skewers.

11 Place the golf ball on the cardboard inside your skyscraper. This gives your skyscraper some weight.

12 Turn the fan on so it blows on your skyscraper. See if your building can stand tall against strong winds!

DIGGING DEEPER

When the wind hits a skyscraper, it is forced in all directions. Some of the wind is pushed downward. Its force is added to the wind already blowing near the ground. This increase in wind force is called the downdraft effect. It makes areas with many skyscrapers seem extra windy. Engineers look for ways to reduce the downdraft effect of the buildings they **design**.

CONCLUSION

Skyscrapers are important structures. They provide a lot of room without taking up a lot of ground area. More skyscrapers are built every year. Engineers work to build skyscrapers that are safe, useful, and fit in with their cities' skylines.

QUIZ

1 What is the tallest building in the world?

2 Skyscrapers never have more than one use.
TRUE OR FALSE?

3 What is a skyscraper's framework called?

LEARN MORE ABOUT IT!

You can find out more about skyscrapers all over the world at the library.
Or you can ask an adult to help you **research** skyscrapers **online**.

Answers: 1. Burj Khalifa 2. False 3. Skeleton

GLOSSARY

architecture – the art or science of building. Someone who designs buildings is an architect.

attached – joined or connected.

curtain – a large piece of cloth that can be pulled across a window or a stage.

damage – harm or ruin.

design – to plan how something will appear or work.

flexible – able to move or bend.

identity – the distinguishing character or quality of someone or something.

lengthwise – in the direction of the longest side.

online – connected to the Internet.

rappel – to climb down the side of a building or mountain by sliding down a rope.

research – to find out more about something.

scaffold – a temporary or movable platform for workers to stand or sit on.

seam – the line where two edges meet.

slit – a narrow cut or opening.

stack – to put things on top of each other.

warehouse – a building or room for storing goods.

May Watts LMC
800 S. Whispering Hills Dr.
Naperville, IL 60540